THE BOOK OF YOUR LIFE

RYAN W. McCLELLAN

RYAN W. McCLELLAN

Circle 5 Publishing Group
9835 SW 84th Street, Miami FL 33173

ISBN: 978-1-727017-052

Dedicated to a great friend, Hector Noriega...
You gave to me; now I give to you. Thank you for your
ongoing support to see me through my college years.
Your hard work and dedication to those around you is
not in vain, and this book is now proof of that...

Preface

"A hero is someone who has given his or her

life to something bigger than oneself"

- Joseph Campbell

When I began to write this book, I found that a key principle of everyday life involves placing yourself as the hero of your own life story. That is what I believe, and if you read these words and the words that follow, you will find that it is not as hard as one may think. In fact, it is rather easy to formulate a life story starring yourself, when no one else is even around!

We all go through times of hardship, as well as times of despair; we all shimmy through life's hurdles, and if we choose to believe that we can be a part of something bigger, we find that life is rather easy! In fact, it is rather simplistic in nature - just paint the broader picture rather than focusing on the little things such as work, love and friendships.

Instead, focus on you – and only you.

This is the key attribute of life: learn that you are worth more than you think, and that the dancing puppets that surround you are merely facades of decadence. They are supporting characters in your book, and you are the hero welding the sword. They may also be great allies, strong and vibrant, and willing to help you grow as a person. We will discuss this in the coming chapters, but first, a bit of history.

I came up with this outlook on life rather easily. I began to realize that much of what goes into writing a book is the same as writing your daily life. What do you do in the morning that culminates the remainder of your day? What do you do throughout the day that causes you to assess the lengthier picture? In turn, what delineates your *own* Three-Act Structure, of which is the central theme of this book? You will read more about that in the words to come, but for now, begin to assess your life's outcome.

What are you looking forward to? What brand new beginnings are awaiting you? These are all questions you have to ask yourself *before* you write your life's tale. Now, do not mistake this for a raunchy self-help book; do not mistake it for personal development. Look at it as a preparation for the future, and a new way of examining the world around you. Again, we can ask questions all day, but in the end it is on you.

And only you.

You must sink your teeth into this novel and truly

begin to see life as a story. That might be the hardest part, as it requires dedication. There is no "easy way" to go about this, and you have to confirm to yourself that you are ready for what you are about to read. If you are going to whimsically brush through these pages with ease, you may find that you are not yet ready for the words that follow. You need to commit!

Does that mean this book is hard to work with? No, but it *does* mean that you have to be prepared for a lot of homework. This means focusing on broad themes such as conflicts in life, a fond emphasis on the Three-Act Structure interplaying into your daily existence, and the many characters that surround you. These are people you may know, or they may be people you have yet to meet. Regardless of their role, they will be playing a big part in your life's chapters.

As a Life Coach (I know, *everyone* is a Life Coach, hence why I refer to myself as a Life *Counselor*), I have seen how many people are in need of structure, and that is what this book entails: quite literally, something called the "Three Act Structure." This will allow you to progress through life's milestones with great ease, but you have to work for it. This is a book about greatness achieved through writing your life in a manner no one else has thought of doing.

I will be the breaker of this rule.

So, do you have what it takes? And why is this book so paper-thin? It is because it is easy to sum up life – really it is. It is not a hard façade to master. If you can learn to adopt this new way of thinking, you do not need more than 100 pages to fill the void, and trust me, there will be plenty of "things to do." You will be developing a Three Act Structure, basing your life on a beginning, a middle, and an end; you will be documenting daily conflicts that increase your chance at success; and you will be figuring out who your supporting characters are (i.e. back-up).

This is a book about life, yes, but it does negotiate itself as a book about writing, too. The individualism of this book will guide you through the process of writing your life in a manner no one has thought of before, and I proudly present this work as a tribute to everyone. They say there is a need for a target demographic or a "buyer persona" in any business venture (yes, this is a business venture; you are the buyer). I firmly disagree. I feel that this is so broad in nature that it is relevant to anybody, anywhere, anytime.

When you have been maintaining abstract ideas as long as I have, you find it is easy to regulate the buyer as a person who can be just about anybody. And, as a Life Coach (sorry, *counselor*), I also have dealt with so many people telling me to find a "market," or to be an "expert" in something in order to achieve success. Again, I fondly disagree. I feel that expertise is calmly represented by that fact alone, of which is the ability to take a concept and spread it across any given canvas, painting a beautiful picture that *everybody* can enjoy, respect, and idealize.

So, without further ado. I present *The Book Of Your Life* to you, your loved ones, and your friends. Feel free to thank me for it, hate me for it, or never make it past the first chapter. Either way, I will feel contented in knowing that I shared an *idea* with you, and that idea is simple: be all you can be, and be the hero of your story. Let us begin to examine how this is done…

CHAPTER ONE

What's In A Book?

"Everyone is necessarily the hero of

his or her own life story"

- John Barth

You might be asking yourself how a self-help book can possibly relate itself to a novel. I am wondering that, too. How can we possibly associate something so broad and so concise as life itself, to the process of writing a book? Well, it is possible, as I will soon prove. As an author of four fiction novels, I have seen the similarities and they are more than just abstract; they are alive, unlike a book (so we would assume).

In life, we find ourselves caught in the web of dissident moments; we have rules; we follow a Three-Act Structure; and we are always in need of new "supporting" characters to make the quest before us a lot easier. But to understand how this book about books (paradox, anyone?) fleshes out, let us first examine what these factors portray, and how they fit into the wormwood that is our daily grind.

When writing a book, an author often uses things very similar to life. We have to abide by a series of rules, such as grammar, spelling, and syntax. Much like in life, we have to make sure that the book is easy to read and equally easy to follow along with. If we were to misspell every word, it would be rather hard to get through it without trepidation.

Just like in life, we have to abide by certain rules that society presents us with. You find out early on in life that running around naked is not in the best of interests for society; you learn to speak a certain way in order to make sure the world around you understands what you are trying to say.

These are very similar to the rules an author follows when writing a book. We have to make sure we allow our book to be readable to others so we can succeed in getting our point across. I am watching television, and I just saw a mob of protestors tear down a Confederate flag somewhere in Washington. See? That is an example of how a book must maintain understandability, of which is very similar to what I just did: *not* cutting ourselves off when a random fact arises itself. This is known as "syntax."

We must also abide by grammar. This is parallel to most societal functions, such as the previously-used example of keeping your clothes on when stepping outside of your home. What happens when grandma goes outside without her robe on? She forgot how to use grammatical logic; it's just that simple.

This is a very important rule to follow, as society and the world around us has certain expectations for us to shadow, and for us to succeed (just like an author requires proper grammar and spelling to get something across) we must maintain these rules with diligence! Otherwise, we fail as a group.

It is easy to see how important keeping our clothes on is, but what about a more abstract concept, such as the way we progress through life? There is also something in the world of writing known as a Three-Act Structure that many people do not realize they follow. This is a broad concept many authors and playwriters claim they have attributed, but to this very day we still account the infamous Aristotle for the culmination of a beginning, a middle, and an end.

Taking it a bit further, in the time of theatrical plays (I remember those), Shakespeare was known to use a Three-Act Structure that tailored itself around tension and build-up. He took the "beginning" and made it a "setting," which is basically when the main characters are presented, as well as the location. It will then proceed to "conflict," where the tension begins to build and we reach our problem at-hand. Finally, there is something called "resolution," which is where the problem will often solve itself, however it is not always a "good" thing.

In recent years, we are discovering more and more about the Three-Act Structure, such as the fact that in our modern day, there is actually something known as a Five-Act Structure, which consists of a "setting," a conflict consisting of two parts: "rising action" and "climax," and a resolution that consists of two steps: "falling action" and "denouncement."

Rumor has it that this was because back when a playwriter needed to keep individuals coming back after each of the three acts ended, they would have to end it with a "twist," leading the viewers into the concession area where they could discuss the oncoming struggle, followed by an impulsive spree through merchandise and concessions.

Though rumors are often outlived.

How does this relate to life? Well, for starters, we know that on a psychological level, we reach formal milestones throughout life – just like in a screenplay. We begin by first introducing ourselves to the world with birth, and we soon begin to accept life for what it is. This is your "setting," where you begin to understand who does what, and so on. You learn that the mailman delivers the mail; you learn how to spell; you learn how to speak...so on, so forth.

In our "conflict" stage, we begin to grow. I find that most people reach the conflict stage when they are either a) beginning a new job, or b) beginning a new family. Though these two cornerstones are not for everyone, and may not *exist* for everyone, the point remains the same: that the "conflict" stage is represented by something occurring that is of great significance to ourselves and those around us.

Finally, in our last part: the "resolution" period, we reach retirement; we let go of our children as they venture out into the real world. In fact, I have found that we go through this varied Three-Act Structure momentously, over and over again, repeating the process. Unlike in a screenplay, there is no "one" moment that defines us; there is no "one" moment that can be designated as "conflict."

In other words, we find that there are dozens of Three-Act Structures that make up our lives, and we have to begin to look at them as just that: steps in a structured novel or a screenplay.

There is also a need to maintain proper spelling. If you do not spell correctly in a book or a written work, nothing will make sense. Threr wll b turblance, as an example (you have no clue how annoying it is staring at a bunch of red lines thanks to Microsoft Word's spellcheck feature, but for the sake of learning I will progress). This is much like in life. If we forget to spell correctly, things get jumbled up.

I like to think of grammar as the manner in which we do something, and spelling as the manner in which we view something. If we do not abide by good grammar, we are unable to perform our daily tasks properly; if we do not abide by good spelling, we lose sight of what is important. Just like when we are pulled over for speeding, we must be vigilant in our attempt to correct our behavior.

If we continue to spell improperly (and in this case, do things that are unnecessary or rude), we do not progress; we stay locked up in chaos and so does our daily life. Just like this very program I use to write, it is always looking for things to correct, and we have to view life in the same manner.

If I kept spelling improperly, this document would be filled with red lines beneath every word, which is not only annoying but is also kind of stupid. I do not know how else to put it: it – is – stupid. Remember to spell correctly, and when you are unable to spell something on your own, just right-click and find the correct version of that word.

What else do we know about writing that portrays itself as a real-life scenario? Well, think back to any book (better yet, buy one of *my* books and think about it) and recall the introduction of what are called "supporting characters." These are friends, family members, and even those we may dislike or disagree with (often known in stories or books or screenplays as "antagonists"). These are "supporting characters" – individuals that play the role of the bow-welding elf or the magically-healing fairy.

At least, if you are comparing to 'Lord Of The Rings." Which I am not, but for sake of argument...

These supporting characters sometimes stay with us; other times, they vanish without a trace. Too often, we find ourselves using them in ways we eventually learn to avoid. We find far too often that friends become enemies, and that enemies can also become strong allies. The point of a supporting character in a book is often to add substance, but in real-life, they find their way into our paths for other reasons, often in a manner of friendship.

A supporting character is someone who not only provides substance; it also allows our stories to be more interesting. Often, we find ourselves lost in the former (or present) lives of them. You will notice that in many books, supporting characters have more than just a "supporting" role; they are shown as living, breathing entities. This not only provides a coax element; it also gives them personalities and stories, as well, and this must be acknowledged.

We see this represented in real life by our friends, but we must remember that just like in a story, there are tales behind them, too. We always need to remember to treat them as human beings and not cushions to throw around when we need them. That, in itself, is what makes them our supporting characters! They are there to help us when we need it, but we must be omnipresent when they need us, too, and we must be constantly looking for chances to assist them in their *own* life stories.

Finally, there is a fond, noble progression in books that we also notice in life. Though we discussed the Three-Act Structure already, progression in writing is a bit different. It means that the book flows from page-to-page, and just like in real-life we notice how momentously every day begins to lead from "conflict" to "resolution," and then back to conflict. This is the one part of a book that often does not mimic that of real-life, as a book often consists of singular moments of resolution, never once continuing or repeating itself (unless a sequel is in the works).

As we will see, there is no "single moment" of resolution, or conflict, or setting. We all face daily challenges, and as we will see through this book, there is daily progression. We wake up; we live our lives; and then we resolve. We go to sleep, and we wake up, only to do it again. This is the message I will be giving to you throughout the following pages: that life is momentous, and though we speak of a desolate comparison between that and the way books and stories progress, there is a lot more to it than that.

Now that we understand how life and a grand novel are similar, let us begin to assess this concept in further detail. Ready for the fun stuff?

CHAPTER TWO

Why Is This Important?

"A mentor enables a person to achieve. A hero shows what achievement looks like"

- John C. Mather

Writing a book is much like living life. There are moments that cause us to pause and re-examine the world that is around us; there are other moments where we have to suffer at the hands of self-disdain; and there are times where we see a pattern forming, paving way a figuratively-themed "yellow brick road" that leads into the dwellings of a higher sense-of-self, humbling us with its presence and equivalency.

Just like in a book, we see that life is balanced on a series of steps, and we realize how important it is to divide life up into something like the Three-Act Structure, where we elect a setting (a beginning), a period of conflict (where life takes its turn down a barren road), and a resolution (when we begin to realize that the conflict has ended; the war is over).

This allows us to move from page-to-page with succession. Though we often fail to look at it like this.

Far too often, we see life as just that: a one-time venture that can lead us in any direction it chooses to. This is not the best way to think of life, in my opinion; we must grab it by the horns and progress as we see fit, based on our own individual or personal values and requirements. In the world of writing a book, progression is important because it provides a solid framework for where we start, where we face a time of hardship (or sometimes even success), and when the closing of said hardship/success ends. In life, we are not often given these opportunities, and we may skip right over "conflict" and go from "setting" to "resolution" with the snap of a finger.

But this is something I feel we could all begin to utilize to our advantage! What if we could all account for where a new setting begins? Would we be able to redefine our conflict? And furthermore, would we choose to resolve, or continue with conflict, adding filler, and proposing a much thicker book that eventually finds itself releasing itself as a hardback rather than a paperback like this one?

Take as an example: you are beginning a new job. You have to introduce yourself to a plethora of new individuals, and must slowly earn their trust. As you walk into the office, you trip and a box full of framed pictures and non-office-ready staplers fly out of your hands! You have just entered "setting," and you must now work your way from "laughing stock" or "new guy" to a higher position, where suddenly everyone you saw as above you is now at your beckoning call! This is the venture we take through the Three-Act Structure, and it repeats itself momentously.

As I had stated previously, we all have multiple settings, a multitude of conflicts, and tons and tons of resolutions. Though even the most detailed novel or screenplay follows a singular path through the Three-Act Structure, in life we often see these steps repeat themselves consistently, and often on a day-to-day basis. Is your morning drive to work a setting in and of itself? Or is it instead represented by the job you eventually reach? When does resolution begin? What defines your conflict? In turn, what defines *you?*

This is what we will begin to identify.

It is imperative that we understand that life is not a linear act, as I will soon discuss. In plays and novels, we rarely get to see the whole story. Usually it will end on a good note, but what happens after the screen fades to black or that final page is read? One can assume a happy ending occurs. Think about a classic romantic such as the infamous "Cinderella" – she finds true love and they live "happily ever after…" but what happens after that?

Does the prince eventually cheat on Cinderella, leading to a messy divorce? Who gets custody of the kids? Why is the prince so moody? Why does Cinderella have such weird slippers? Am I talking about the right story? You can see my point here: life does not progress like a novel or a movie or a play; it consists of plot twists that we may not ever get to witness if it were put down on paper.

Tales and fables forget to tell us the full story. In real life, we consistently move through plot twists that lead through the setting, the conflict, and the resolution, and back again. Is it always in that order? What if we progress from setting to resolution, skipping the conflict? This can actually occur. You may go through a series of events that lead from a setup to a moment of realization or truth, skipping haphazardously over the conflicting period. But does this make it any less (or any *more*) significant?

We also see a theme of supporting characters in our lives, just like in a book. And as we continually write in this book, adding in plot twists and allocating new resources, we take on the role of "rising action." We may choose to divide up our conflicting moments; we may be products of our setting. This allows us to figure in our allies and delineate our antagonists, or those facets of our lives that cause pain and hardship.

In the end, we owe it to our family and friends (our supporting characters) to recognize their importance in our lives' books, and how much trouble they have guided us away from. In turn, we can appreciate them as allies we have gained during our "setting," or perhaps as products of our "conflicts," aiding us all-the-while as we battle through our daily lives.

Just like in a book, we must often dare ourselves to venture into new places to locate good-hearted supporting characters. It is not always a group of people we already know; I often find family and former friends are a part of your setting rather than conflict. This is because this book should mark a new moment in your linear existence: the attribution of knowledge, and a new way to look at your life in the heart of dissertation and in reverence of incentive.

How do we identify our supporting characters? Look around you. Who are your key players? Do you have a solid network of friends who are always at the ready when you are down-and-out, or do you have a strong network of family members who are able to assist when you fall? In turn, who is missing? There are several roles to fill, of which *you* and only you must be willing to venture onward for.

I like to think we all need at least two of these roles in our lives, depending on what type of person we are. Are you the sword-welding hero? If so, hand-to-hand combat may not work in every situation, and for long-ranged combat (laugh at your own content) you need the arrow-welding elf; for it is in those moments where you are face-down in a puddle of your own sweat that you require a magic wizard to heal you.

Obviously, this is rather figurative, and why I chose a fantasy novel is beyond me. I may use "Lord Of The Rings" as a broad example, but for the sake of the written word, I call upon Gandalf for strength and Frodo for courage to explain my point.

In other words, we all need variety in our cast lists. Your supporting characters should not all be the same, but who am I to dictate how you live your life? What if you choose to view this as a Stephen King novel, such as "The Dark Tower?" In this case, the Gunslinger seems to function alone, except for that one kid that seems to help him out on occasion (doesn't he die? Did I give that away? Sorry).

Often, you may find you are The Gunslinger, and you do not need a cast of supporting characters...but then what do you call your enemies? That is the other aspect of modern life we can all relate to: there is an *antagonist*, or a bad guy. This "bad guy" can come in many shapes and sizes. It can be a negative boss, a peculiar offender, or merely a situation. I do not think your choice of antagonist should rely solely on a person; often, we find situations are our enemies.

What is an antagonist? In a story, there often *has* to be a bad guy. But unlike in stories, real-life does not always consist of an antagonist we can clearly identify. A situation can be an antagonist; a location can be an antagonist; and still, we may find our antagonist *is,* essentially, a person. How do we handle this without derailing the train? Here is some quick advice before we progress in this tale of wonder: know thy enemy, but also understand that just like our supporting characters, that person (or location, or situation) may have a lot on their plate, and this causes them to take out their negativity on the hero.

We often find in stories that the antagonist has a tragic beginning. "The Wizard Of Oz" (both versions) portrays an evil witch as the "doer" of all evil...but what do we know about the witch? She melts with water, which does not make much sense, considering the fact that there is a lush forest to wander through, meaning rain is most likely occurring (then again, the trees also throw apples at people), but we also know her past. Though there are more than just movies about the "land of Oz," such as several books that actually are quite frightening, we do know much of her "wickedness" is based on jealousy.

Another grand example of an antagonist is that

creepy sister in "Alice In Wonderland." Another quest ruled by what can be insinuated as jealousy, we often find that there are back-stories to even the most evil of antagonists. And often, they are quite rational. This is much like in real life, where there was once a good side to someone (or some*thing*) that creates tension. In stories, this is meant to invoke a story – without bad, we cannot recognize the contrasting element of good. This goes for everything in our daily lives!

We must learn through the lens of time that the evils in our lives have a tale to tell, as well, and we must recognize it for what it truly is. We must acknowledge that there is pain in other people, as well, just like we see in stories. It is no mistake that the antagonist often comes with a tale; often there is no correlation, but this still means we have to understand our antagonists to figure out ourselves.

Finally, we see how powerful we are as the "liver's" of our lives. We learn to roll with the punches, and hopefully we begin to see ourselves as more than just human beings; we recognize our installation as heroes of our own life story, and this provides a sense of acknowledgment and self-value. We begin to realize how complicated our lives are in comparison to the complications of others, and it often pays off with a realization that we are not in as bad a shape as we once pondered until we meet the wicked witch (and find out *her* story).

Can you imagine how much we would all be able to accomplish if we saw ourselves standing upon such a brightly-lit canvas? I think that realizing our potential as heroes consists of two steps: reliving our settings, and using it to fight through conflict and toward resolution. If we were to begin to see life as a book, knowing that we all hold a different-colored pen, imagine the possibilities! We could reinvent the wheel; we could find resolution, allowing us to pass on the crown to others in the wake of our successes!

In this sense, by holding the pen, we are the detailers of our own existence, and you are the hero of your own story! That is what this book is about: realizing how to write yourself into your own life, outlining who you are as a person, and what role you play in this book we call "life." Shall we progress onto the good stuff? I think so. Are you ready?

Let us begin to reinvent the wheel!

CHAPTER THREE

First Steps Toward Success

"Love of glory can only create a great hero;

contempt of glory creates a great man"

- Charles Maurice de Talleyrand

As a Life Counselor, I have found that it is often best to start at the beginning, and to account for what situation we are in at the present moment. I urge you to take out a pen and a piece of paper, and draw a single line on the X axis. If you do not know what the X axis is, take a brief look below (for sake of understanding, I have included five vertical lines of which we will use in the coming pages):

X_____|_____|_____|_____|_____|_____X

Before anything, identify what your conflict is. Where are you right now, and what are you trying to accomplish by reading this book? Are you hoping to achieve a better career, or are you trying to develop a family? Are you in the works of graduating from college, or are you trying to find a job based on said graduation? Or are you simply lurking in shadow?

Take out your pen and draw five vertical lines as

shown. First, draw one where you are right now; mark it with a vertical line and draw a path from it; write "Now." Then, draw two lines behind it and two lines in front of it. Your job is to now figure out what your setting encompassed (the two lines behind you) and what your goal is (the two lines in front of you).

You have just begun a story.

The two lines behind you represent the "setting;" the present moment represents "conflict;" and the two lines in front of you represent "resolution." Consider the two lines behind you. What led you to the situation you are trying to work your way through? It is important to know your past, just as much as it is to know where your future begins. By designating a setting, you are able to look back upon the timeline and examine what caused you to progress from "then" to "now." This is your setting.

Then, the two lines that follow in front of you represent "falling action" and "resolution." Just like we discussed, there are two stages in resolution: falling action (the ending of the conflicting moment) and the actual resolution itself, often defined by the ending of the story. It is very important to figure out exactly where in "conflict" you are. Are you in "rising action" or "climax?" The best way to understand this is to answer the following three questions:

1) Are you building up to something?

2) Are you leaving something behind you?

3) Are you in the wake of something big?

If you answered "yes" to any of the above questions, you may be in "climax," which means that the build-up to your present situation has ended, and you are at a point in conflict where you are on your way to the final resolution. Honestly, it is not hard to figure out where you are on the timeline. All you have to do is figure out if you are in a state of calm lucidity or if you are in a state of broad excitement.

If calm, you are in "rising action." I figured this out one day when I was taking a short walk around my block. The psychology behind this is rather interesting to me: "rising action" usually builds up to something, whereas "climax" is often already in the midst of struggle. When we are building up to something, our brains are naturally hardwired to place us in a state of serenity. This is part of survival instinct: a concept that consists of two parts of the human experience.

Sympathetic nervous system: a part of the human nervous system that activates by exciting us so we can make it either toward or away from a given threat. Often called "fight or flight."

Parasympathetic nervous system: a part of the human nervous system that activates by calming us so we can rest, usually in the midst of oncoming danger. *Not* "fight or flight."

So, how do you feel about the situation you are in? Are you excited or indecisive, or are you instead lucid and calm? Better yet, are you angry or complacent? This will allow you to truly understand what part of "conflict" you are in. Why does this matter? Well, you have to initiate *where* on that timeline you are. We know that conflict is amidst; otherwise you would not be reading this book. However, that line you drew designating the present moment needs to be either a) rising action, or b) climax. There is no "in-between."

If in "rising action," you are calm, and your end goal is to figure out how to reach "climax" so you can finalize with "resolution." If you are in "climax," you are in the midst of a struggle, and you need to figure out how to get to "falling action" so you can comply to "resolve." This may be more than confusing, I know, but what did you expect? You are reading a book about how the Three-Act Structure is alive and well in the human experience. Of course it's confusing!

Now, try hard and think back to two dynamically-relevant moments in the past week, month, or even year since the conflict began. Mark them down on that timeline behind you. This is your setting, and it will help you by acting as a guideline of what caused what. What led you to where you are right now? Is it something that can be redone or reworded? Recall our discussion about life being a book: you hold the pen, so begin to rewrite the setting in order to find your way through the mesh of contest.

Often, there are too many moments to count, and we need what I like to call an "extended" timeline. This means that perhaps five or ten situations led you to where you are now, and this often comes in the form of a life story where there is a *lot* of progression. In this scenario, you have been building up to your resolution over weeks, months or even years. I like to think we have two types of "life" timelines: *extended* timelines and *short* timelines.

Extended timelines consist of intense progression. You have been working through your conflict over a broad period of time, beginning with a momentous setting (example: birth) and leading up to a conflict (life!). Finally, your resolution reaches fruition when you have a family and your kids go off to graduation. This is in contrast to a short timeline, which we are going to be discussing throughout most of this book: day-to-day routines beginning with you first waking up (setting), conflict (your daily life), and resolution (of which can come in any form, just like conflict).

Once you know what kind of timeline you are

going to be working on (both are beneficial, but for sake of brevity you may want to isolate just one type), you can move onto the next step, which is easier said than done (yes, it gets *weirder*).

The next step is to try and locate your supporting characters, of whom must be capable of helping you through the present situation. But first, as we had discussed, not every conflict is a bad thing. Starting a new job can often lead to a career, of which does not seem too much like a bad thing.

However, when we recall our past experiences with conflict, we see that even the best moments – whether those that catch us by surprise or those that are planned to an absolute tee – consist of some form of struggle. Take as an example something we have *all* experienced at some point in life: our first date.

I use this term broadly because *no one* has ever had a successful first date; it is a fact! No matter how well you think it went, when you look back upon it, you will cringe at how awkward every moment was; how many things went wrong; and how vibrant conflict is, even when in the context of a "good thing." However, the first date we go on is by far the biggest example of how the Three-Act Structure interplays into real life: there was a setting (in my case, about two years of working up the nerve of asking the person out on a date), a conflict (the date itself), and a resolution (if you were lucky enough: a first kiss).

As you can see, the concept of this book correlates to more than just a lengthy experience such as life itself; it can be crunched together into evenly-spaced and singular moments of existence, and that is why I urge you to use what you are learning throughout this book on a day-to-day basis. If you can take five minutes out of your day to identify the setting, potential conflict, and an end goal (resolution), you are setting yourself up for success. You will *always* be prepared for the worst, and you will have a game plan for every day, facilitating a better life.

This is the key to a good existence.

Once you have figured out where you are on that timeline, begin to outline your supporting characters. Whether team members at work or friends you have known since birth, these are the characters in your book who hold something you do not. We see this represented in writing far too often: the supporting character often holds a different weapon than that of the main character, i.e. you. If not a different weapon, they hold a different viewpoint or even an opposing or different outlook on how life is meant to be lived.

This allows you to succeed when you least expect it. If you are performing a short timeline, you are accounting for the individuals found throughout your daily routine. If you are performing an extended timeline, these are often people you have known for quite some time, and they have most likely already been involved in your life's struggles.

Begin to write their names down, followed by a creative (albeit, weird) character description, much in the same manner as an author would do.

This can look something like this:

Name – Bringer of Good – Always has snacks.

Name – Always of Use – Hardheaded and strong.

I chose to give a nickname for each, but this is not being graded; write down whatever you want. As long as you indicate the person and the values they bring (even something as simple as always having a snack when you are hungry), you have done your due diligence and now have a list of those who can and *will* help you through your journey.

Now, for the remainder of this book, I will be using the Five-Act Structure in place of the formerly-used Three-Act Structure, and they will bounce back and forth. This is simply because sometimes it is best to use the Three-Act Structure in certain aspects, and the Five-Act Structure in other aspects. So, keep up.

Now we have figured out where we are in the Five-Act Structure, who our supporting characters are, and what values they bring. We have also identified what our conflict is, and what we are fighting for.

Onto the next chapter!

CHAPTER FOUR

Battling Through Conflict

"Peace is not absence of conflict. It is the

ability to handle it by peaceful means"

- Ronald Reagan

As we have seen, there is a dual-edged sword when we speak of the term: "conflict." It is not a fact, nor plausible, that in every play (or in a book, or in a screenplay) we come in contact with, our "conflict" is solely defined as a bad thing, and the same goes for the opposite of "resolution."

Not every ending is happy, both in writing and in real life. We have to remain vigilantly-prepared on this journey we call life, and constantly try our best to keep track of it using *notes*, as it is often the times we focus on the most that have conflict that is something we grow from, with a resolution that makes you a better person. So, let's begin to prepare!

First step: realize that every day will have a new twist. Just like in a book, every day consists of a series of small, indiscernible and unrecognizable moments where we battle at the hands of a wicked boss, or a situation that may seem less caustic, such as a bad drive to work. These are moments we need to allocate as plot twists. What do we do about a plot twist? Well, we have to first decide if it is good or bad.

Second, we must learn to roll with it.

When we are writing this life journey, we have to make sure to realize that plot twists are often the moments that cause us to grow the most. When the character becomes victim to a sudden attack, they learn who their true friends are (and, equally, who their enemies are). This is just like in real life. Who is standing beside you when the bad occurs? Who is standing there as the opposition? These are moments we do not prepare for, and there is really no way to.

But we are able to isolate who is with us in this journey, often unexpectedly. Were any of your supporting characters you mentioned at your side? If not, where were they? And who else joined in on the conflicting moment to assist you? Begin to write down on a day-to-day basis: the number of conflicts you experience, and the type of conflict you are experiencing. I like to think there are three types of conflict that are omnipresent in real life: victories, failures, and neutralities. We either win, lose, or none of the above. That is speculative, however, based on your individual outlook on how life is lived.

You should begin to write down all of your daily conflicts, and look for a pattern. Do you see a lot of moments correlated around a certain person or a situation? And what precedes it? Do you constantly call people names that lead to a dire confrontation? And what kind of confrontation is it? Is it physical, emotional, or mental? Who is the winner? These are all questions you can write down so you can begin to isolate a pattern in your conflicting moments.

I urge you to keep what I call a "Conflict Journal," or a notebook where you map out daily conflicts. Do this for ten days, and see if you can locate any common variables. Do you tend to always find these moments at home, at work, or at school? Do they happen in the morning, the middle of the day, or when you are closing up for bed time? If in the middle of the day, what causes it? Are you maybe hungry, in which case it is wise to contact that friend on page 59, that "always has snacks?" (I told you they would be of use) and ask for a quick fix to keep you on-arms?

When we know what we are facing, and how to

handle the situation correctly, we are able to win the battle, thus fueling us to also win the war that represents our daily lives. Keep this journal going for as long as you can, and every three days, take a look at what was written down. Just like in a book, write down three important facets:

1) The place

2) People involved

3) Conflict present

As you can see, we are allocating a setting, supporting characters and the conflict in question. You can make this as close-ended or as open-ended as you want. I would say the more detailed, the more likely you are to find common variables that will point you toward success. This is a great way to keep track of life in order to determine when and where you find your conflict the most! Trust me, it will come up later on.

Patterns are very important to note; they tell us *how* we end up in a specific situation, allowing us to eventually learn to avoid them - only *if* we are smart enough to keep track of them. Many people just move through life without ever realizing there is a pattern to their conflict, and that is not okay. As human beings, we have the ability to isolate the variables behind a conflict, and use it to turn the tides.

Second: know what kind of conflict you are best at. In a book, we often see the main characters battling fights they need help with. But what happens in life when we do not have our supporting characters beside us? We need to be able to understand how to avoid confrontation when we are "outnumbered," and run in the opposing direction. In other words, when we find conflict we are not capable of battling alone, and our supporting characters are nowhere to be seen, we must learn to back up!

Once again, this is where putting things down on paper is necessary. We can see what patterns emerge from our conflict period and it allows us to begin to avoid those situations we consistently lose at (and which ones we are capable of fighting).

Third: know when to call for back-up. A lot of people seem to abide by the most basic instinct we have: the fight-or-flight reaction. There is a saying in Martial Arts: when you get hit, your mind will only register two thoughts – back the heck up, or get the heck *in*. We see this all too often in daily life when rush hour traffic hits, especially in Miami.

Everyone has a gut demarcation to honk the horn the moment the light turns green, never giving a passing chance to the person in front of us to put down their Happy Meal and press down on the gas pedal. This leads to a maladaptive society.

This instinct, ironically, states that we will either soar from a situation with broad wings, or stay and fight...but what if you are outnumbered to a point where even Liam Nielson could not win? You have to learn that at certain times in our existence, we must either retreat from the conflict, or find someone to help us. It's just that simple. Know when you are about to be kicked in the butt, and know when to put the sword down and run away.

This may save your life. I made this mistake once when I was robbed. Three guns pointed at my forehead, my first instinct was to push the gun out of

RYAN W. McCLELLAN | 71

my face; I was cocky, and that cockiness led to an escalated situation where I was suddenly face-down on the ground, screaming for help. This is an example of a time when I should have retreated from the conflict because instead, I chose to escalate it. That word: "chose..." It brings up a good point.

Know which battles you can fight (even with back-up). Pick and choose them based on their severity. We often forget to assess a situation before rushing the danger in a silhouette, and we find all too often that we get our butts kicked based on this. Human beings are temperate (albeit, fundamentally stupid) creatures, and we like violence. This does not necessary indicate a bad thing, but it does show that our instincts far too often misguide us.

How do you override an instinct such as this? Re-read through your daily Conflict Journal as often as possible, and see which conflicts led to victory and which led to utter failure. Indicate the *severity* of the failure. Were you face-down in the dirt, or were you walking away with a messy shirt? Is this the life you wish to continue with? Because if there are repeat instances of the same thing occurring (and the same repetitive consequences), maybe it is time to stop doing it. Shame on you, shame on *me*. That simple.

Yet conflict is not necessarily a negative thing. Sometimes we like to feel conflict is a bad experience, and why not? The name itself portrays intense negativity; how could it possibly be good? Well, think about what we experience during these small moments of battle (often with words exchanged or simply a situation we experience, such as a bad day at work). We feel hurt, pain, indifference...all of these things are psychologically known to cause growth.

When I first started playing guitar, my fingers had yet to develop the callous necessary to push down on the strings without pain. I remember how painful and excruciating it was to play a single song, let alone a set! But after a while, this conflict between my fingers and the guitar strings began to settle, and callous formed. Now, I can play better, faster, and without pain. This is a great example of what conflict does to us: it strengthens us on the inside.

But remember that sometimes we still push too hard upon those guitar strings, and even with strong callous, we are inviting pain into our lives. The human experience is represented by repeated successes and repeated failures, and that is why I find keeping this Conflict Journal so momentous, as it allows us to reflect on our daily lives in taciturn. We begin to see the patterns of either good or bad behavior, and it is then that we can reinforce the good, and tame the bad, never letting it happen again.

When you do something right, reward yourself for that victory. If you get a raise because of hard work, or you are in-line for a promotion, pat yourself on the back. If you *lose* your job based on a heated argument with your boss, write it down and return to it at a later point; I guarantee it will conjure up negative emotion, and you need to use that to your advantage as otherwise, we never grow.

When there is a negative consequence for a certain behavior, we have to reflect on it; when there is one that is *positive*, we have to reward ourselves. This is called "behavioral modification," or "behavioral reinforcement" in the world of psychology. The concept was coined by a man named Ivan Pavlov.

Before he would feed his dogs, he would ring a bell, and before long he began to notice that the dogs would salivate when they heard that bell ring. It was the beginning of a new psychological theory called "classical conditioning," meaning that even without the food being delivered, the dogs became wired on an intransient level to salivate, associating that ringing bell with the promise of food – even when no food was actually in their presence.

What if we could all learn to modify our behaviors in such a manner? Would we be able to cause a subconscious desire to do the right thing? This Conflict Journal you are keeping will serve as an experiment, in my eyes, as if you are able to reward yourself every time you recollect a positive conflict, perhaps you will begin to associate that conflict with reward, and the opposite with a slap to the face (quite literally: when you reflect on a bad experience, slap yourself – hard! You'll never do it again, trust me). Though I advise against actually *doing that*.

Now, sometimes we have to allow conflict into our lives in order to grow from it. Often it is instinct to run away from a bad situation when in reality, we need these times to strengthen us. Growth is facilitated by negativity. When you prick yourself on a cactus, you eventually learn to stop touching the darned thing because guess what? You will keep getting pricked! This is the same in life. We need to accept conflict into our realm of thought, and look at it as a momentous experience that allows us to grow.

In writing, there are some instances called "uh-oh" moments. At least when *I* write. These are times when we experience great turbulence in the story, and when the conflicting moment literally makes us say: "uh-oh." Rarely in the story does the main character run away from the situation; I have never written, nor read, a book where the character turns around and runs in the opposite direction. This is because in stories, a single principle is contemporary: fear often leads to dire conflict, but conflict leads to progression – something very important in life.

When these "uh-oh" moments occur in real life, such as finding out you just sent the wrong order to the inventory department, you have to stand up and face the fire. If you choose to avoid it, two things have to be coincided: 1) you will eventually find it, as it will catch up to you, and 2) even if you escape its grasp, you are not allowing the fire to burn you, which facilitates advancement and evolution! Our first instinct is to run, but the fight-or-flight ethic I spoke of prevails: when in danger, we either rush the danger or we grow wings to soar away from it.

Now, this does not mean grab a loaded gun. We have to pick and choose our battles based on common sense. What happens when we are outnumbered? If you are finding yourself lacking in supporting characters when conflict occurs, it may be a wise idea to run. But the point is simple: often we have to allow conflict into our lives to grow as people.

Mapping out daily conflicts on a sheet of paper is quite beneficial. Once you have begun to isolate what common variables are present when you reach an "uh-oh" instance, you can locate a pattern that allows you to prepare more for it when it happens. Example:

you seem to be running late for work a lot. What is causing this from occurring? Is it a shower that perhaps takes too long, or are you merely sleeping in? Knowing what *causes* the conflict is just as important as knowing how to handle it.

This "Conflict Journal" will be isolated in further detail in the coming chapters. For now, begin to practice writing down in a notebook the chain of events that led you to a positive or a negative conflict. Then, begin to reward yourself for the good, and slap yourself for the bad! With this sense of positive (and negative) reinforcement, as we have previously discussed, we grow as people, and we begin to find which patterns are beneficial to us.

Again, knowing what *causes* your conflict is more than important. Rather, it is a facet of our existence that we need to also reinforce, as otherwise we become instinctive, which often fails us. The human brain consists of parts – there is a forebrain (where the frontal cortex is located, of which controls reasoning and impulse control) and a hindbrain (where our most basic instincts rest). We need to begin to tame the hindbrain from reacting, and begin to accentuate what makes us human: the forebrain, where all of the stuff that makes us good people is set in place! All you have to do is *reinforce it!*

It's that simple.

CHAPTER FIVE

Rising Action Vs. Climax

"For good ideas and true innovation, you

need human interaction, conflict,

argument, and debate"

- Margaret Heffeman

As stated on page 53 or so, you are currently in the conflict stage, whether you know it or not. The question is, what part of the conflict stage are you in? I gave you a very well-rounded tip: identify if you are calm or vivacious, as our brains are hardwired to detect whether we are closing in on danger, or if we are in the midst of it. If you are calm or even lucid, you are in what is called "survival mode" and your mind is preparing for a climactic moment; you are in rising action. But if you are feeling active or energetic, chances are you are at the climax stage.

This is a pseudotheory, i.e. it is not proven by science. In fact, I made it up. However, the written word does not lie – if you choose to believe it. In this sense, are you working toward climax or are you working toward resolution? If in rising action, you are moving into a climax, and you need to prepare for the danger that is surely headed your way.

So, how do we prepare for it?

First, begin to assess the situation. Are you aware of what is coming? Is a big billing report due, of which you have not prepared for? This is a hard one to delineate, as this could lead you into either rising action or climax (you may be preparing for climax, or you may already be in the thrust of life, waiting for the worst to occur yet still hoping for the very best).

Regardless of what part of the "conflict" stage you are in, you need to go back to that notebook of conflicted moments and see if anything relevant prior to this has occurred. Have you ever been late on assignments at work before? If so, what did you do that worked, and what did you do that did *not* work? This is why I said to be as detailed as possible: you never know when it will come in handy down the road. Next, isolate a way to *resolve* the situation.

Again, what in the past has worked? If no exact or directly-relevant situations in the past come up, use some common sense. Remember, your job is to move to climax so you can further that toward falling action and resolution. If you are in the climax, your job is to get through it without closing that second act of the play with an intermission that is sour to the taste. However, if we have learned anything from the written or spoken word, it is that in the event of a negative climax, we still have a chance to resolve it later on, perhaps in the third act.

Let us examine rising action. Rising action is the part of the story where things are beginning to grow cloudy; the skies are beginning to grow dark, and the sun is slowly but surely dampening. In this period of time, your mission is to begin to prepare for the climax, which is when things truly become rocky. Of course, this is all if you are experiencing what I call a "negative conflict," or one consisting of a negative experience. Not all conflicts are negative; some can be positive, as well. When you see yourself in positive "rising action," you are actually doing the opposite.

Rather than seeing cloudy skies forming, they are slowly disappearing, and the sun is beginning to shine once again. This is when it is best to try and figure out what your situation entails. In rising action, it is often the best time for you to begin to understand what kind of climax you are going to be experiencing. Begin writing down what has gotten you to this point. Was it good? Bad? Neutral?

By knowing your past, you will be able to better understand your future, and you will be able to guide the pen across the page in a manner that facilitates future involvement and further growth.

This is when it is imperative to begin to document your routine in broad detail. Begin to write in a Conflict Journal: all of the things that occur in your present moment. Does a new acquaintance appear? Write it down. Is there a new promotion now being offered at work? Write it down. Rising action is the best time to document your findings!

Now, once you have a rudimentary understanding of identifying rising action, you will find that it is easy to predict a negative climax, i.e. the hero is about to fall off of a cliff, and it is your job at this point to contain the situation! Some climax moments are good, such as a new baby or an unexpected job opportunity. Other times, it can manifest itself as a chaotic whirlwind of despair. Ever have one of those "periods of time" where everything bad you could possibly imagine suddenly comes to fruition? Well, that is usually found in the climax of a novel or a play, and if you can learn to detect it before it happens, you can avoid a stressful situation by simply rewriting the last plot twist. How do you do that, you ask? Start by thinking long and hard about the history of whatever event is unfolding upon you.

Recognize the key points like we did earlier; look for clues; try and decipher the past as if it were a relic held in bronze stone. This will allow you to pinpoint spots upon a timeline, as we had discussed earlier, playing the role of the detective and unraveling threads of string you may have forgotten about. Once these moments are identified, you can then begin to assess what can be done to prevent that moment from derailing your entire existence.

Other times, you will want the climax to occur; this is part of life, and to live through pain and turmoil is a facet the hero of every story needs. Often, a dire plot twist in a negative direction is what facilitates enough anger in the hero to fuel a vivacious action scene! I urge you to take those notes seriously. Your "conflict journal" is essential to your success in life, as it allows you to isolate similar and equally-momentous experiences you may have had earlier, and to use them in a beneficial manner.

There is another way to do this. If you recall that time-line you drew up at the beginning (which we will soon finish, by the way), try to recreate it as often as possible. Sometimes we react differently to an "event timeline" over a bunch of notes, of which require calculation and a keen eye. If you were to draw a line on the X axis, pinpointing two events that got you to where you are now and two events that lead to the next act, you are in good shape.

Draw that line, introduce your setting (what got you to the moment you are in now), and then indicate two other moments that have yet to occur. Figure out what needs to be done to reach resolution. If you made a mistake, how can you fix it? This may seem like common advice: find a solution to the problem. But when you think of life as a self-written book or a play, you may also find this process not only becomes easier, but is also a lot less stressful.

Now, if the climax is negative, and you *know* it will be a negative situation, this is called a "negative climax," and it is something you can seek to avoid before it occurs. When you are able to recognize a negative climax, the best thing to do is to skip over it and reach resolution quicker. But how the heck do you do that without interfering with the story?

I like to think that though this is an option that can be solved by simply reliving the setting and rewriting it so the climax is resolved, it is often best to let the hero suffer. Why is that? Well, as we discussed, the point of this is not only to map out our lives; it is also to grow. When we skip over a negative climax, we find ourselves never truly growing from the situation. We learn based on clues, and much of this process is based on things we do not want to *ever* occur.

However, remember that often there is a plot twist waiting to unfold. If you hold the pen, and are in charge of the situation, make that climax positive!

Easier said than done, right? Well, you really only have two options here: suffer through the results of the climax and see how it turns out, or try and turn it into something that it is not. This can be done by allocating a different path for you to take. If you are realizing your job is about to perform interviews with every staff member to review progress, and you *know* your progress has been subpar, you might want to take the criticism. From there, learn from the mistake. If the situation is more dire, such as this being your third strike at work, what else can you do?

For starters, you can be prepared! Know exactly what your reasoning behind that lack of progress is; have a plan set in place so that you know exactly how to "rewrite" the situation so your boss understands!

When preparing for a *positive* climax, do not always get your hopes up. We all know how life can throw twists and turns our way, even when on a broadly-lit and intangibly-straight road. Think of this process as driving in the dark: yes, you have your headlights, and perhaps you even know the route you need to take to get to your destination. But what lurks in the darkness around you? It is unseen, and we can all agree that life is random and haphazard.

So, here are a few tricks to maintain that climax.

1) **Know thy enemy.** If you have an oncoming

negative climax, prepare yourself with every ounce of strength in you. You may face some dire opposition, and the climax may leave you tired, worn out and shaking, but if you know what you are up against, you will succeed.

2) **Create a game plan.** Use that "conflict" journal to write down the facets of the upcoming climax that are negative. If nothing else, you can learn from the experience by documenting it for later use. You never know when history will repeat itself, and in stories, it often does.

3) **Resolution is coming!** Even in the event of a climax that is negative, remember that it must be reached in order to scale the ropes of falling action, which is followed by (you guessed it) resolution. As we discussed, that is not always positive; a resolution is simply the end of something and can actually make things worse. But if you play your cards right and set up a strong preparation for the parts of the Five-Act Structure that aren't your cup-of-tea, you will

get through it and will actually grow from it!

Life is a journey we all have to learn from. All we can do is try and look at it in a manner that is reasonable and also, sophisticated. When we look at a situation in accordance with the rules that we have identified (proper grammar, a Five-Act Structure, and a strong group of people around us that can act as supporting characters), failure is never truth.

In other words, when you reach resolution, make sure to remember that another Three or Five-Act Structure is on its way, and you need to be vigilant in your understanding of it. Knowledge is power, and the best way to sully through life is to retrace your steps. Remember to always check your blind spots, and designate where something begins; take notes about your life, as if you were writing a story (which you are); know that there will be both good and bad.

This, in essence, is success in your very hands – quite literally – and you control the outcome. That is why I find this method of thinking so valuable and so useful: it gives a sense of control over our daily grinds, allowing us to focus on the past in order to designate a better future. It is part of the human experience to retrace footsteps, but many of us choose to avoid this kind of mentality.

This is mostly because we are creatures of habit: we go about our daily routines without ever thinking that, if we try, it could be accomplished differently.

In this sense, we must learn to avoid closeminded thinking and embrace a new way of doing things. This will lead all of us to success...though many will try and fail, it is a game of numbers: sometimes we will reach a wonderfully-epic climax; other times we will find ourselves caught in the phase of resolution, wondering how such a crummy ending to the play could ever occur. But that is the point!

We have to learn to suffer a little bit, but to also look back on what we have done in those situations to succeed later on when the time calls for its review.

CHAPTER SIX

Allow The Climax!

"The harder the conflict, the more

glorious the triumph"

- Thomas Paine

Remember our discussion about our supporting characters? Well, they now have a purpose: they serve as a support system for when the climax turns out to be a negative one. However, first let us discuss why allowing the climax is imperative. First and foremost, think of how often we find life turning out as completely the opposite of what we expect. Despite the many planning tools we have discussed, we know that not all days will turn out in our favor.

This is when your supporting characters come into play. When life turns out to be unexpected and unpredictable, we need to make sure we have a solid grasp on both others around us to help when we fall, as well as a tried-and-true sense of optimism about the outcome of said moments. A wise man once told me: "Life is not linear." Examining the word: "linear," we see that this is very true: not everything we expect as "good" will be good, and not everything we expect as "bad" will turn out bad. In this sense, we need to be prepared for either scenario.

Why is this chapter titled "Allow The Climax?"

Well, let us look back upon the last chapter: we need to live through all of those negative moments in order to calculate how to go about life the *right* way. If we do not let ourselves suffer every now and then, we fail to grow. But this chapter is not all about suffering through even the worst moments; it is about how to live through those moments correctly.

By now, you should have begun to work on many daily timelines and many daily conflicts, as well as the resolves that follow in their wake. Have you seen any patterns? Have you noticed that often a negative climax results in a positive resolution (and vice versa?) This is the magnitude of life: it is truly not linear, and the waves of progression move much like tectonic plates beneath us: they do so without warning, but what have we learned about them?

When a tectonic plate grinds against another, it can cause an earthquake or a volcanic reaction. However, we also see that most of life's great mountain ranges were built on a foundation of (you guessed it) tectonic plates grinding against one another! This is a great example of how something that also topples buildings creates things that, later on in life, we can climb on top of to gain a better viewpoint of the world around us.

With this in mind, allow the climax, even if you have predicted that it will turn out as "bad." That word, in my opinion, is overused and overrated. "Bad" sometimes allows us to grow, to thrive, and to eventually reach a moment of resolution that changes our lives forever. *But*, we need to make sure we do not let every climax turn out negative. If a life is at stake, or you foresee it causing you to lose your house, your best bet is to intervene.

But how do you do such a task? Well, remember our timelines. Examine your setting. Are you setting yourself up for a pattern that results in a negative consequence? Did you screw up a billing report that will lead you to a climax where you lose everything? This chapter is about allowing *certain* climaxes into our lives, but to also learn to avoid the ones that cause a catastrophic end result.

In plays (and books, and screenplays), the climax can come in any form, but it is often one of two things: good, or bad. It is rare to find a climax that is neutral; that allows for no character progression, and people will soon begin to abandon the book or leave the theater. The only thing we can use to benefit ourselves is knowing just that: that it will either be a good thing or a bad thing; the rest is up to the writer. This is why allowing the climax to unfold (whether good or bad) is essential, because it allows us as human beings to move through it and into resolution.

How boring would that book become if you read 100 pages only to find that the main character has no tangible consequence for what was accomplished in the setting? The point of life, and the point of a book or a play, is to maintain an interesting perspective. Otherwise, what keeps you locked in and reading until the ending when the good unfolds?

We must also note that the climax is not always in the middle of the book; sometimes we have to read 200 pages before we reach the resolution, of which serves as a climax. Look into a movie called: "Buried," starring Ryan Reynolds. I use this movie as a broad example because it shows how often we do not recognize when the conflict occurs and when the resolution begins. It begins in darkness. Reynolds finds himself locked in a box and buried beneath a thick layer of sand, and all he has at his disposal is a flashlight, a pencil, and a cell phone.

The ending is rather caustic, and he dies at the end (I had to give away the ending because otherwise, I cannot stretch out my point). There are multiple moments of dire conflict here, such as the emergence of a snake that crawls into the box (how a snake got twenty feet deep in thick sand is beyond me), or the onset of the sand now filling the box. The ending is not happy, and there is no resolution; there is no "one" moment of conflict; and yet I keep watching it, despite the fact that the Three-Act Structure is indiscernible and nowhere to be seen.

In fact, the entire movie is one giant climax!

This shows how not every story follows a linear path, but it is found within this fact that the movie remains of interest. We have to make sure we understand that life is not a linear facet, and can move in any direction – even away from the very resource we have been discussing. Our Conflict Journal may be quite messy; our timelines may follow no direct progression. But they are still of value.

Imagine if this movie *had* followed a structure. Would it have been just as interesting and ominous, or would it have proven predictable and even less renowned than it is? We can see that the climax can come in many shapes and sizes, and may occur sporadically and without any given warning. This is why I feel the proposed resources I have provided (timelines and Conflict Journals) are even *more* relevant because they allow us to see its effects.

I want you to now begin to write in your Conflict Journal: timing. Yes, include the day and time. This allows you to see how unpredictable and sporadic the story you are telling (i.e. your life) truly is. If we succumbed to a timeline that represented vertical lines that were spaced evenly apart from one-another, we would be blind to the chaos of life. In turn, we would not be able to define when one period ends and another begins. In a screenplay, there is a golden rule: the 17th page is the beginning of conflict.

We also note that the standard screenwriter is told to keep their work at exactly 90 pages, and this is because a minute of screen-time is represented by a single page. I feel that this is why many plays, books and movies lack unexpectedness, and that is perhaps what makes them fun: they sully us from how life *truly* occurs, providing a sense of fantasy and illusiveness. But life is not like that; it will have a setting that may only last five minutes, a conflict that spreads itself across months at a time, and a resolve that may never even show itself.

Bringing us back on topic, allowing the climax means more than just struggling through conflict; it also means that we must be willing to keep track of it when it occurs. This further exasperates our ability to see patterns. Maybe your settings never occur; maybe you begin in conflict. But in the end, the resulting effect will *always* consist of a single attribute: life is interesting because of its never-ending sense of disarray and disorder.

Want an interesting life? Let the conflict occur. Just

remember to learn from it, and when you can, document it so you can return to it later, and perhaps you will begin to find ways that *would* have prevented it from occurring or leading to a negative resolution years after it occurs.

We discussed patterns earlier on, and this is relevant in allowing the climax. In the end, everything leads to something. We have the beginning of our something, the ending *to* our something, and an "in-between" period that can consist of just about anything. *Anything.* Does that not get your heart racing and your blood pumping?! That is the whole point of this experience: allowing the climax means that you are simply allowing life to occur! The only difference is, with the new knowledge we have learned through this book (and I thank you, as I have learned just as much as you have), we can begin to send it in any given direction we desire.

Trust me.

Though the hero needs both positive and negative climaxes (and will always be accountable for more than just one climax in a given lifetime), you can do yourself a favor and have a routine in place that will mnemonically trigger a defense system inside of you that brings everything back to homeostasis. This can come from a trick called "mindfulness." When you-know-what hits the fan, some people duck; others stock up on high-absorption tissue paper and tons of soap. In other words, train your mind to focus on the moment; figure out things to do and a routine to follow in the event of turbulence.

I often tell my clients to write (and laminate) a list of things that make them happy. I have heard of everything from "working out" to "going to a gun range." This list is very important to have - not only because it assists in progressing through conflict; it also has psychological value. The more your brain experiences a specific routine during negative times (and bear in mind, it is already proven that the human brain can tell when we are emotionally in danger), and the more consistently that routine works in our favor, the more likely it will begin to attach to the survival response within us, of which is known to calm us (or ignite us) during hardship.

It is called "behavioral reinforcement," as we had discussed, though if you are doing it to yourself, the term is better off represented by "behavioral modification." In essence, you are training your brain to activate this routine on a subconscious level, simply by practicing it every time you enter a period of stress or emotional dissidence.

We are, unfortunately, very much in-tune with predictability, and this method allows us to push through that horrid (or equally eclectic) climactic moment with ease when it is not of a good nature (and when it *is* of a good nature, we have to learn to bask in it, because the next one may not be so great).

If you can attribute this attitude and routine into your life, you may be able to allow that climax to occur without fearing the worst. All you will have to do is consult that laminated sheet of paper, and engage upon it. This may not always work for you; sometimes our negative moments are far too difficult to face through routine. *But*, it has worked in the past – just like in our many settings. We must find ways to utilize this process to our advantage.

CHAPTER SEVEN

Reaching Resolution

"The changes in our life must come from the impossibility to live otherwise than according to the demands of our conscience – not from our mental resolution to try a new form of life"

- Leo Tolstoy

Wow. Talk about that last chapter culminating tears! But the good news is, most stories end with a good resolution; it is what makes us feel better about that horrible conflict. This is much like in life: we face turmoil, but we can use it to our advantage. When the conflict is not of a good nature, it is our duty as founders of this way of thinking to make sure we have planned for a good resolution!

But how do we do that?

For starters, we have already learned to examine our pasts. Before, we were examining our setting. Now, it is time to examine our conflict. The first question to ask is: was it expected? Often, the victories we planned for turn into horrible failures, and it is these moments where we further understand our resolutions. When we reach our resolve, we have to isolate what variables got us there. That, in itself, is the essence of existence.

Often in a story, a negative conflict results in a positive resolution, and vice versa. Though of course we are not condemning ourselves to fairy tales here, this is one way to look at things: how was your conflict? Was it what you expected when you planned out your mission, or was it the exact opposite? If positive, how can you keep it from back-firing on you when you reach the end? Furthermore, how do you know when the story is ending?

Resolution is perhaps the one part of the Three (or Five)-Act Structure that we are *always* able to recognize. When we have changed, grown, fallen, or in some cases: have stared death in its cold, blackened eyes, we are at resolution, and the battle has ended. There is no way to describe how resolution occurs, but we know when it happens. I sure did, and so will you.

Reaching resolution is when the hero reaches some form of conclusion. Sometimes it is found in the defeat of the antagonist; other times, it is found in powerlessness over a situation that we finally grow to understand as just that: powerlessness. When we learn from an experience, whether it ends or not, we have reached our resolve!

Now, you have to make a dire decision, as my tale

lasted three months yet I have already stated on many occasions that our lives are not fixated on moments of duality, nor are they always found in the delicacy of three months. They can come and go on a daily basis, and sometimes something as simple as falling asleep after a hardy day is, in itself, resolution. Another great example is this chapter, which is the resolution of this book; we are at the end of a great journey, but what we choose to do with it is on *you*.

It always has been.

How will you handle your ending? Will you fall victim to your own sword, or will the antagonistic forces around you govern the ending? Do you have the strength to do what I did by ending something that represented a cornerstone of my life: my first relationship? Or will you cower in fear, and never write that angry letter to your boss, or your ex-lover, or yourself? This is completely up to you. You have to decide how you wish to end a dangerous climax, and it is often best to prepare the ending before the setting even begins! This is often done in writing: the ending is written before the beginning is culminated.

Remember to look for patterns, as always. I honestly cannot stress that enough: isolate patterns in life. This will tell you what kind of resolution is on its way, and what direction you need to pivot in in order to reach a state of conclusive happiness. Far too often, we let our instincts govern the ending. This is part of the human experience: allowing the ending to write itself, when in reality we have complete control of the outcome, regardless of the situation.

As a Second Degree Black Belt, I have come to realize that the loser is often the one who gets winded first. When we compete in tournaments, we are taught to breathe with every strike. When we are out of breath (and in figurative terms, out of ways to reach resolution), we cannot make the next move, and that is when opposition strikes hardest.

In essence, control the outcome.

Xenophon of Athens, a man who was once a great yet misunderstood philosopher in the times of Ancient Greece, once said: "You know that neither numbers nor strength give the victory, but that side which, with the assistance of the gods, attacks with the greatest resolution is generally irresistible." In other words, and as confusing as that may be, life is not meant to be looked at in the light that I am proposing. Resolution does not come in the form of any variable other than your own wellbeing.

Now, we have discussed that life is full of a multitude of conflicts, but we cannot look at life that way; we truly can't. I may be preaching against my own advice here, but in reality, when resolution hits, we know about it; it is human instinct to understand when the end of something has come and when the beginning of a new chapter culminates.

When a mother births a child, we can all agree that that is the end of the pregnancy; we have reached resolution. We also know that a common hormone called prolactin is sent to the mother's neuronal circuitry the moment the placenta is officiated, enabling the development of breast milk. When we die, our bodies are subjected to rigor mortis because the physiatry's most fundamental chemical: ATP, is no longer there (when you die, you stop breathing, and without oxygen, ATP cannot be produced).

In the end, resolution is hardwired into our lives, and it is just like the resolution of any given aspect of life. This is the part of the book when I tell you: resolution will come; you will *know* when it comes. There is no way to tell how it will come, or when it will come. Rather, you will just know. But it may take some time for that to occur. When we find our resolutions, we have a single choice to make: we can accept it and begin a new setting, leading to more conflicts and other resolutions...or we can remain vigilantly stuck and withered in the moment.

That choice is up to you. But if you try and force resolve, you will never truly reach it. You have to be willing to let go of the battle of conflict in order to truly win the war. It is almost as if we must give up a part of ourselves, even if the resolution allows us to gain something new!

We must be willing to release ourselves from conflict, in this case. Without that key element, we are unable to move into resolution. Once again, this is the part of the fabric that this book resides within that I have no true answer for. I cannot tell you how to reach resolution except by saying: "Simply finalize the conflict." That is about all of the advice I can provide to you. But will you choose to let go of the conflict in order to gain resolve? And is there any fear within your soul that prevents you from it?

The one and only thing I can say with grace and sincere compassion is this: remember that the moment resolution is reached, a new setting begins! The question is: how will you let yourself pass through the resolute stage and into a new setting? This really depends on the impact the battle of conflict took from you (or what you gained from it).

Often, if the battle was bad, the resolution will be good; at least, that is what we like to believe, as stories and plays typically end happily.

But on occasion, we find a resolution is just that: the end of something relevant to us, and we must find a way to give up that moment, to seep through its vibrant cracks, to stain the fabric of our existence, and to release all of our energy into the "next step," which is, in itself, a new setting. How do you prepare for resolution? You don't. That is the one part of the story where you do *not* plan. You wait patiently for it to occur, and when it comes, accept it for what it is.

Once you have reached resolution, document one last thing in your journal: what form that resolution came in. Was is as you expected? Did all of the assets you wrote prior to the ending of all endings actually happen, or were you miles away from where you intended on being? This, in itself, is probably the hardest part of the system we are working with, as it shows you how futile your prior efforts may have been. You may have been expecting a happy resolution when in turn, you experienced one that was full of negativity. How do you live with yourself at this point? How do you carry onward?

For starters, you learn that this system works! Truly it does. You will see that time is on your side, and that you are capable of predicting the future – with practice, it eventually becomes second nature.

CHAPTER EIGHT

Final Words

"Information is the resolution

of uncertainty"

- Claude Shannon

RYAN W. McCLELLAN | 125

So, we reach the end. How does it feel knowing you have accomplished basically nothing? It is true! This book was *nothing*! But you learned from it, didn't you? I can tell by the smile on your face that you did. And that is where we come to our conclusion: the notion that we have actually just begun to work this new outlook on life. When dealing with this kind of thinking, you have to be very careful to *not* let it interfere with your life; let it come naturally to you.

Again, I will not bore you with a long "farewell," as you have plenty of work to do – including plenty of thinking, plenty of writing, and plenty of *doing*. This is the kind of book where you have to take action for it to work; you cannot count on life to toss you a lot of opportunities, as that is the exact opposite of what I am trying to attribute to you. Rather, you have to get up and go find them. It's just that simple.

So, share your feedback; write a review; take to the streets or social media and tell your friends if this was helpful to you. If it was not, I urge you to do the same. Remember, life is in your hands now; it is a matter of how you play your cards that will culminate success or failure. Will you play the hand, or will you challenge the bluff? Will you face the fire, risking shame or persecution, or will you turn and run in the other direction? And in essence, what happens when your "conflict" does not indicate a good resolution?

We went over a lot in this book – much of it being the Three and Five Act Structures (the two are rather interchangeable in a lot of ways). We have related it to life, but can you turn the metaphorical (and the rhetorical) physique of this concept into a reality? Can you live by it, breathe *based* on its functioning, and in turn, write your life story with a smile on your face as you pass by that last chapter?

I am happy to have written this book; it has been rather fun! But that is not the same for you. I hope it was whimsical, to say the least, and worth whatever price Ingram decides to make you pay for this, but it does need to be taken with a sense of dedication. You must *commit* to what you have read here, and to use it to your advantage as you ride your white horse into the battle that is our everyday existence.

In reality, the only advantage is *you*, and how you choose to define your conflict, how you choose to write your supporting characters, and essentially turn yourself into the hero of your life story. I will not lie and say that I am the *first* to say "live as the hero of your life story," but I am certainly the first to describe it in such a manner, and I do hope that at the very least, you can take a reluctant step forward and use this idea in your journey to health, happiness, and success. If you wish to backtrack, do so.

Read through every paragraph; buy a four-dollar pack of highlighters and mark all of the important parts. Or, ignore this, waste your time (and money), and never reread this, despite it being written solely for that purpose: to be reread, and to be mastered.

And if you need some guidance or assistance in any of the motions we have attributed here, contact me; my information will be on the last page. I am a Life Counselor, a Business Consultant, and a man who lives by a single code: forget what is good and bad, and understand that "right" and "wrong" are much more imperative to a long and healthy existence.

So feel free to reach out.

Good luck!

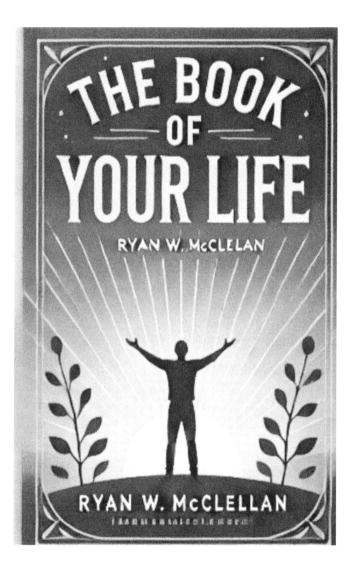

PLEASE LEAVE A REVIEW!

Being an author can be tough. That is why I am including a QR code below so you can leave a great review if you enjoyed this!

This should take you to the Amazon.com page, where you can leave a great review, a bad review, or whatever you feel is right!

ABOUT THE AUTHOR

Ryan W. McClellan, MS was born in vibrant Miami, Florida. He has been weaving stories for as long as he can remember. He has six captivating books gracing store shelves and a collection of free eBooks available to readers worldwide. McClellan has established himself as a versatile and passionate storyteller. His journey as an author began at just seventeen, when he penned his first novel .It was a milestone that cemented his lifelong love for writing. Over the years, his dedication to the craft has earned him recognition, including awards for his compelling stories.

Made in the USA
Las Vegas, NV
30 December 2024